30 Seconds to
PROSPERITY

Inspirational Quotes
to Begin Feeling and
Experiencing
Prosperity *Right Now!*

By
RYAN A. HARRIS

Copyright 2009 by Lighthearted Publishing, LLC All Rights Reserved. No portion of this book may be reproduced or transmitted in any form; mechanically, electronically, holographically, or by any other means without written permission of the publisher, except for brief quotations for inclusion in a review.

Printed in the Unites States of America

Lighthearted Publishing
3401 Adams Ave., Ste A
PMB 204
San Diego, CA 92116-2490
Phone 800 619-9080
Fax 858.430.3592
Email: info@lightheartedpublishing.com

Limits of Liability and Disclaimer of Warranty:
The author and publisher shall not be held liable for misuse of this material. This information is strictly for educational, inspirational, and informational purposes and does not constitute psychological or business counseling or advice.

Appreciation

I would like to express gratitude and appreciation for the following people who have contributed to this book and to my life.

Sabrina Harris, my beautiful friend and mother to my son, who is a living example of how to walk in the light. "In this world, but not of it" has never been more appropriately applied than to you. Thank you for your tireless efforts, incredible sense of design, and endless hours of work with no tangible reward other than a sincere "thank you!" You've helped more than you'll ever know!

My parents, Donald "Duck" Harris and Nancy Bennett, for their constant encouragement, love and support, and for being such wonderful examples of insightful, warm, and loving individuals, each in their own unique way. I love you both and appreciate everything you have done for me.

Esther and Jerry Hicks, for bringing forward the most useful and practical life teachings on the Law of Attraction. Jerry's ability to ask questions and Esther's ability to bring forth the answers from Source Energy has been a blessing for mankind, and me personally, for which I feel overflowing appreciation.

Ed Rush, business and marketing genius extraordinaire. Thank you Ed for your inspiration, motivation, genuine service, and no-nonsense, down-to-Earth approach to business and life. It's been a pleasure following in your footsteps.

Special thanks go to Jennifer Devlin, Laine Harris, Albert Muller, Donna Kozik, James Malinchak, Wayne Dyer, Louis Hay and Hay House Publishing, Rich German, Joanna Withey, Kamala Devi, Tara Brennan, Steve Prussack, Craig Garber, Greg Milner, and everyone quoted in this book. Thank you!

Help Others Realize Abundance and Prosperity! - "Share this Book!"
"Makes a wonderful and thoughtful gift - any time of year!"

30 SECONDS TO PROSPERITY
Inspirational Quotes to Begin Feeling and Experiencing Prosperity *Right Now!*

Life can be a challenge, and with today's busy lifestyles, it is very easy to get pulled off the path of abundance and natural well-being. This gem of a book contains quotes from some of the world's most expansive, gifted thinkers and "accomplishers" who are intimately familiar with prosperity and abundance.

Each page contains a powerful quote along with additional commentary by the author, and reading this book is an excellent way to instantly get your energy back in alignment with prosperity, so all of you actions and efforts are done in the right spirit, with the right energy, to produce maximum results. Give the gift of prosperity and abundance to your friends, colleagues, and loved ones, and enjoy the tremendous cost savings.

Special Quantity Discounts
5-24 Books just $9.00 each
25-99 Books just $8.00 each
100-499 Books just $7.00 each
500-999 Books just $6.00 each
1000 + Books just $5.00 each

To place an order, call (800) 619-9080
or visit www.30SecondsToProsperity.com

INTRODUCTION

This book is for everyone who does not right now, in this moment, feel "prosperous" and wants to change that in 30 seconds or less. But what is prosperity? It is a feeling, that could be described as a combination of appreciation, contentment, desiring more, trust in the process and the inevitability of success, patience, positivity, and joyful expectation, all rolled into one.

Prosperity does not mean financial wealth. For most people, financial wealth is a large component of prosperity, but it's not everything! In truth, prosperity is an attitude. It is combination of attitude, feeling, mindset, and a state of overall wellbeing within an individual, being recognized and appreciated for what it is. It is not about being rich, but ironically, the people who have strive to cultivate the feeling of prosperity invariably end up being financially comfortable as well.

Because it is a state of mind and a way of being, not an outward thing that can be measured, it can be "obtained" in just seconds. This is done by shifting our emotions, our thoughts, and letting go of our resistance to "what is". It is ceasing our feelings of resistance and struggle to let our natural wellbeing come to the surface.

It is said that people with poor dietary habits are really

Introduction

only "one meal away" from being back on track to optimum health. Getting back on track begins with taking the first positive steps to implement actions based on a new intention.

In the same way, because prosperity is a state of being that is not dependent on outward circumstances, a person can shift into prosperity consciousness almost instantly. That is why the title of this book is 30 Seconds to Prosperity, because we can shift into prosperity energy as soon as we choose to!

It's not easy to make that shift without positive outside influence. So I created this book of quotes to provide inspiring words of encouragement, to share with you that prosperity is not some far off and hard to obtain set of financial circumstances. It is simply realignment with our natural state of joy, accompanied by positive expectation, gratitude, and being fully present in the moment. You can have this NOW.

The quotes in this book are design to help quickly shift you into this prosperity mindset. It isn't always easy because your habitual thought patterns and self-defeating behaviors are so ingrained. But it can be done by everyone over time, by continually improving their thinking degree by degree, day by day, until a new thought pattern, one of abundance and prosperity, becomes predominant.

About the Selection of Quotations

Enjoying strong and meaningful relationships, being comfortable in your body and environment, contributing as a member of your community, rendering service to others, enjoying physical health, feeling spiritual vitality, and enjoying financial abundance, all of these are aspects of true prosperity. You should strive for balance in all of these areas.

Notice that financial abundance is last on the list. But because so many people emphasize financial abundance in their concept of prosperity, I have included a number of quotes that deal with entrepreneurial success and wealth building.

I chose quotes that pleased me, that conformed to my beliefs and values in the hope that they would resonate with like-minded individuals. I make no claim that these quotes are Ultimate Truths. They just bring me comfort and help me instantly shift into the feeling of prosperity, and it is my hope that they have the same impact on you.

I have included quotes on overcoming adversity, motivation, the Law of Attraction, and the importance of declaring our life's purpose. While not all of the quotes are about prosperity in the narrow definition of the word, I selected them based on their contribution to creating a broad description of prosperity, as well as their overall ability to inspire, uplift, educate, and remind us about how close at hand abundance and prosperity truly are.

After each quote I have added some commentary to provide one perspective or interpretation, but it is by no means the only possible interpretation. Each quote has impact, meaning, and value to each individual according to their state of mind, prior experiences, and beliefs, opinions, and outlook on life.

Concentrate on the quotes that uplift you, empower you, and resonate with you. Dwell on them, try to capture the spirit and meaning of each as you interpret it, and carry these feelings with you throughout the day. Your ability to shift into a prosperity vibration will increase dramatically, and you will start to see changes in your circumstances to match the change in your inner circumstances.

When you feel relaxed, uplifted, and inspired, take any and all action that feels appropriate. Only take actions that you think will move you closer to your goals. When the action feels forced, laborious, or like drudgery, that is a sure sign that you have shifted out of a prosperity and abundance mindset. In that "misaligned" state, almost all action you take towards your goals will meet with extremely limited results, so strive to work towards your goals while in a positive mood, with an air of excited anticipation, and patience.

Let prosperity flow to you in its own time. It cannot be forced, but it can be accelerated by eliminating any thoughts or emotions that are not a match to the qualities of prosperity: desire, surrender, faith, relief, and joyful expectation. I hope you enjoy these quotes as much as I do, and revisit them as often as you need to "fan the flames" of abundance, prosperity, and spiritual wellbeing.

"There is no way to prosperity, prosperity is the way."
– Wayne Dyer

Most of us have been programmed to believe that we are supposed to get happy by earning as much money as possible to buy material things, and those acquisitions will make us happy. And just maybe, if that happiness coincides with wonderful relationships, complete health, and meaningful work, then we will have chased down and caught "prosperity". We will have won!

But nothing could be further from the truth.

Feelings of prosperity are the CAUSE, not the EFFECT. Choose them now, then you will enjoy the entire journey, and surely everything good in life will come your way as the effect of feeling prosperous right here, right now, despite the "facts" of your life.

> "In order to experience everyday spirituality, we need to remember that we are spiritual beings spending some time in a human body."
> – Barbara DeAngelis

Most people assume that we are mortals striving to be spiritual. This alternative take on the arrangement is empowering, and hints at our true capabilities. If we choose this belief and operate from this basis, then we are instantly empowered to take control of our lives in incredible ways.

As spiritual beings, it becomes difficult and pointless to argue for our limitations, and gives hope that we can indeed achieve anything that we put our minds to. Prosperity should be a simple affair for spiritual beings, and for those who adopt this belief and attitude, it usually is.

"A man is not rightly conditioned until he is a happy, healthy, and prosperous being; and happiness, health, and prosperity are the result of a harmonious adjustment of the inner with the outer of the man with his surroundings."
– James Allen

James Allen here reinforces the concept that prosperity is a state of mind in which mental and emotional resistance to the present circumstances is lowered. When our resistance and struggle with "what is" ends, the result is calm, and peace of mind.

Life gets "fuller", with richer experiences, and a full awareness of the present moment can take place. When the inner and outer worlds aren't opposing each other, the desire for more feels good, natural, and unhurried - pleasantly anticipated.

> "The size of your success is measured by the strength of your desire; the size of your dream; and how you handle disappointment along the way."
> – Robert Kiyosaki

As individuals, we alone are in control of the "size of our success", so have you decided how successful you want to be? Have you quantified it, and written it down? Have you etched it in your heart?

Once decided, there is bound to be temporary disappointment along the way, but knowing this will help you to respond to it objectively and positively, so that disappointment just becomes a mere bump in the road on the way to success.

"Everything you've ever desired is being lovingly held in escrow for you. When you consciously and intentionally shift your energy (vibration) to match the energy (vibration) of what is in your escrow, the Universe will knock itself out to bring you what you desire. It is law!"
– Abraham
(paraphrased by the author)

Wouldn't it be nice if the nature of the Universe was such that everything you ever desired was yours for the asking and nothing had the power to prevent it from coming to you, except you? And that it came to you as soon as your nature and essence completely matched its nature, or essence?

"Be thankful for what you have and don't get angry or resentful about what you don't have. Many people around the world are not as fortunate as you. Remember, as long as you have good health and safety you have everything. Not money, cars, fame, or job status. Without good health and safety, nothing else seems to matter."

– James Malinchak

Malinchak here is pointing out the two most important things that we should always be grateful for, and to focus on – our health and safety. If you take these two things for granted, all of the wealth in the world won't mean anything to you. By just recognizing how important these are, noticing that you have them, and letting yourself feel gratitude towards them, you will unlock the energy that creates true prosperity. Not only will you feel better, but you will begin to attract more of everything that is good into your life.

"Desire is the starting point of all achievement, not a hope, not a wish, but a keen pulsating desire, which transcends everything. When your desires are strong enough you will appear to possess superhuman powers to achieve."
– Napoleon Hill

Many writers attest to the power of the "burning desire". Although current scientific instruments are not yet capable of measuring thoughts and thought patterns, it won't be long before we find out how the quantum physics works to explain this "mystical power" as completely "natural" and "utilitarian". If we keep in mind the Barbara DeAngelis quote on page 10, the "superhuman powers" line takes on a whole new significance.

"Whatever you can do, or dream you can, begin it! Boldness has genius, power, and magic in it."
– Johann Wolfgang von Goethe

This may be my favorite quote in the collection, just on "style points" alone. At some point or another all of us have wished to possess incredible powers, to control the forces of magic, to be geniuses. Is this realistic, or just a child's imaginings?

According to Goethe, the simple act of dreaming, setting an intention, then taking that first step to realizing the intention instantly gives us these powers. Is it true? Does it really work this way? Find out yourself! Dream a big dream, feel the vastness of it, feel all of the potential glory wrapped up in it, and then start implementing a plan to achieve it! Find out!

> "Prosperity is whatever YOU decide it is. Don't let anyone else make that decision for you."
> – Ryan Harris

Our western culture has made prosperity and financial success synonymous. They are not. Prosperity is a feeling, not the acquisition of things. Some of the richest people in the world long for escape, for simplicity, for freedom from responsibility. And many of the people who have those very qualities of life long for the financial riches, not appreciating their freedom and peace of mind.

Neither is right or wrong.

Once you understand that prosperity is a feeling, a way of being, then you can decide what type of lifestyle and possessions you build around you to support that feeling. It's up to you. Don't latch on to someone else's desires or definition of prosperity, including the descriptions in this book. Create your own definition that serves you, then begin to create your reality based on that definition.

"If I'd had some set idea of a finish line, don't you think I would have crossed it years ago?"
– Bill Gates

Sage advice from the richest man in the world. Recognize that life is a continual process of growing, expanding our horizons, and making new choices based on our previous experience. We never stop growing. And there is no limit to the degree or depth of prosperity we can receive.

Thinking that there is some magical point in our future where we can suddenly stop doing anything and just rest on our previous accomplishments is a mistake. The moment we do this, we start stagnating, and diminishing.

Set high goals, and look forward to when you reach them, a point at which you will set new greater goals. Look at every accomplishment as the starting point for a new set of choices, a new set of accomplishments.

"Every subject (including prosperity) is really two subjects: There is the subject of what you are wanting (abundance in all areas of life), and there is the subject of its lack. Dwelling on either subject creates vastly different energies, and your focus on either produces vastly different results."
– Abraham (paraphrased by the author)

It is important to recognize and learn to follow this "every subject is two subjects" guideline. Many people get caught in a spiritual trap where they think they are focused on what they want, on what they are working hard to achieve or experience. But in reality, they are unknowingly focused on the lack of what is wanted, and the harder they try, the further away it gets because they are holding themselves apart, on an energetic and vibrational level, from what they are wanting.

Awareness of this possibility is half the battle. But instead of trying to monitor your thousands of thoughts, let your emotions keep you aware of which side of the coin you are focusing. A focus on the lack of what is wanted *feels bad*, but a proper focus on what is truly wanted, *feels good*. It really is that simple.

> "There's enough for everyone. If you believe it, if you can see it, if you act from it, it will show up for you. That's the truth."
> – Rev. Michael Beckwith

There are enough resources and "stuff" to go around. Your prosperity will not detract from someone else's prosperity. If you believe that it will, then you will naturally feel guilty about being prosperous, which will keep it away.

Remember that there is no better way for you to help someone else be prosperous than by setting an example by feeling prosperous yourself, being comfortable with it, and having peace of mind. Your example will be a beacon for others to help them find their way to prosperity. You will not even have to say a word about the subject to be an inspiration to others.

> "Your most precious, valued possessions and your greatest powers are invisible and intangible. No one can take them."
> – W. Clement Stone

This quote can be interpreted in a few ways, and everyone will read it a little bit differently. But the thing that I am reminded of is that our material possessions are not the most valuable things we own. Most of us buy insurance for our physical assets, but we fail to protect our intangible assets.

Our thoughts, beliefs, attitudes, and wisdom born of past experience are our most valuable asset, so protect them wisely.

Every time we open ourselves up to negative influences, whether they be people or influences brought in by the mass media, we give up a little bit of these assets. In time, nothing would be left. So be very aware of what you allow yourself to take notice of, and dwell upon.

"Content makes poor men rich; discontent makes rich men poor." – Benjamin Franklin

Contentment is a feeling at peace and relaxed about your present circumstances. That doesn't mean you wouldn't like to see those circumstances improve even further, but being content does demonstrate that you are able to relax, enjoy the single continuous moment of now that makes up your life. It's an expression of gratitude for everything that has come your way so far.

Be OK with what IS, and you will feel and be content. Don't worry about getting "stuck" with what you have, never getting more. Life is constantly changing, and it is guaranteed that your circumstances will change. Being content and feeling as good as possible guarantees that overall your circumstances will change to a condition that you'll view as "better".

> "If we had no winter, the spring would not be so pleasant: if we did not sometimes taste of adversity, prosperity would not be so welcome."
> – Anne Bradstreet

Bradstreet is speaking in her poetic way of "contrast". Few people recognize and appreciate the incredible value of contrasting experiences and desires. By experiencing the opposite of something we desire, it helps us to clarify our desires, focus on our desires, and have a greater appreciation for what we desire when it comes into our experience.

The simplest example is the enjoyment of a meal. Doesn't a meal taste the best when we are very hungry? And water refreshes most when we are a little thirsty. But how many of us can say we have developed an appreciation for being hungry or thirsty?

In the same way our (hopefully temporary) focus on the absence of something helps to strengthen our desire for it. Recognize the value of the contrasting experience and let this quote serve as a reminder to help you relax and keep a positive focus on the subject that you do want.

> "As sure as the spring will follow the winter, prosperity and economic growth will follow recession."
> – Bo Bennett

All things work in cycles, and we should recognize that relatively "harder" economic times as a nation are perfectly ok, they are expected, and they help consolidate and motivate business. Recession is a necessary step towards future growth, just like winter is a necessity before spring can arrive. So recessions should be recognized for what they are – a foretelling of times to come of greater prosperity, and should therefore be appreciated.

But always remember (despite popular belief) that you are in control of your future, and you do not have to participate in any national or international recession if you opt not to. Likewise, you can opt-out of national prosperity as well if you choose to focus on lack or limitation. The choice to have a personal recession is just that – a choice, and it's your choice to make - the moment you truly believe it is.

"Entrepreneurial success and wealth creation, as well as wealth attraction, require a willingness to risk and experience failure and the emotional resiliency to recover from it quickly, decisively, passionately, and persistently." – Dan Kennedy

Recovering from failure isn't easy for most of us. Being willing to face failure doesn't mean you have to risk getting beaten up by the world, it just means you have to have the right mindset, a positive attitude, and perseverance. If you experience setbacks that you cannot spring back from quickly, you will waste time, waste energy, and deflate your feelings of prosperity for no good reason other than self pity. The key is to not take it personally.

A relationship can fail, health can fail, a business can fail, sometimes all at the same time, but we do not have to think of ourselves as failures. Don't personalize the failure. When you remember that every failure sets the stage for a greater success, and remember the value of contrast, you'll see that failure can be an *incredible blessing.*

> "Those who speak most of illness have illness; those who speak most of prosperity have it."
> – Abraham

This is an oversimplified, but complete explanation of what the Law of Attraction is, and how to put it to work for you. Just talking about prosperity may not be all that is required to achieve it, but focusing on its opposite – lack, scarcity, and poverty, is a sure-fire guaranteed way to keep prosperity at bay.

Dwell on, take notice of, and speak about only what you want. This may sound simple, but we have all developed patterns of thinking that are self-defeating and highly ingrained. Establishing new, healthier patterns of thought takes time and discipline, but it is an enjoyable process and is a very important undertaking. Learn to focus only on what you want and you'll make the Law of Attraction work for you to experience abundance and prosperity.

> "Prosperity is a way of living and thinking, and not just money or things. Poverty is a way of living and thinking, and not just a lack of money or things."
> – Eric Butterworth

If the inner world creates the outer world as all of the greatest mystics, sages, poets, and philosophers have said it does, then your patterns of thinking and therefore your patterns of living are the most important consideration. Once again, recognize the true cause and effect in any prosperity or poverty situation.

Both prosperity and poverty are states of being. Which one is predominant in you? Almost all of us want more money, but is the feeling of prosperity in you right now? If not, begin to shift your thinking which you can do in just seconds, by choosing thoughts that feel better. Better feeling thoughts <u>always</u> lead to increased prosperity.

"If there's a will, prosperity can't be far behind."
– W. C. Fields

Humor is good for the soul. Don't make a big deal of prosperity; after all, it's just a feeling that is yours for the asking. Take time to live in the moment, laugh as often as possible, and trust that everything is happening the way it should. W.C. Fields knew how to enjoy the moment! If you don't see the joke in the quote, read it again!

> "Move out of your comfort zone. You can only grow if you are willing to feel awkward and uncomfortable when you try something new."
> – Brian Tracy

The funny thing about our comfort zone is that it isn't all that comfortable, because it constantly shrinks. If we do not face our fears, stretch ourselves, and challenge ourselves just a bit more each day, or comfort zone gets smaller and smaller. Everything starts to become uncomfortable! And the more it shrinks, the more we are not at ease, which could also be called a state of dis-ease.

The cure for this state of dis-ease is to intentionally put yourself out there into growth inducing, uncomfortable, scary situations. Face your fears. Don't feel you have to plunge right in, you are allowed to start with baby steps, small battles. Sprinkle in the occasional leap into the scary void. Any stretching of your comfort zone will keep you moving in the right direction of personal growth and an increasing sense of ease and prosperity.

**Learn to become still. And to take your attention away from what you don't want, and all the emotional charge around it, and place your attention on what you wish to experience."
– Rev. Michael Beckwith**

This is another great quote about what should and should not be the object of your attention. Yes, the problems and struggles you face attempt to demand all of your energy and focus, but if you focus on the problem, instead of the idea and energy of the solution then you will not get the results you are seeking.

You are aware of what you don't want (lack of money, scarcity, ill-health, etc.), and probably have been aware of it for a long time. You probably have an incredible amount of emotional energy invested in the problem, and this energy will take form as more of the same problems. It is time to put your attention on the opposite of what you don't want – what you DO want (abundant health, plenty of money, incredible relationships, etc. Build up a positive emotional charge around those things and watch your life begin to transform for the better.

"Prosperity is only an instrument to be used, not a deity to be worshipped."
– Calvin Coolidge

Here Calvin Coolidge refers to financial prosperity, cautioning us against greed and being hungry for power over others via financial wealth. Money or wealth should not be worshipped (despite the attempts of the marketplace to convince you otherwise), but recognized for what it is - energy - freedom, a tool to be used to increase health, happiness, freedom, self-expression and to carry out service to mankind.

"True prosperity is the result of well-placed confidence in ourselves and our fellow man."
– Benjamin Burt

Confidence is a prime ingredient when new intentions or goals are created. A lack of self confidence indicates a lack of understanding of the true nature of prosperity, and how to bring it about. If you do not have confidence in the fundamental rules of the Universe, such as the Law of Attraction, then of course you will feel uneasy, powerless in the face of inevitable large-scale changes and shifting climates and conditions. But when you have this understanding, you feel a sense of trust in the order of things which allows us to relax and proceed with dynamic energy.

If you lack self-confidence, recognize that self-confidence is the result of ingrained, habitual thought patterns, and these patterns of thought can be changed in relatively short order. This is accomplished by making self confidence and personal growth a highest priority. Continually challenge your longstanding beliefs about yourself and replace them with a view of yourself as a strong, confident person who is on a path of continual improvement.

> "Whenever a negative thought concerning your personal power comes to mind, deliberately voice a positive thought to cancel it out."
> – Norman Vincent Peale

Recognizing negative thought patterns regarding prosperity is the first step, but without then replacing them with helpful, better feeling thoughts that shift you towards the feeling of prosperity, you will not actual feel prosperous. It is difficult to be self-aware enough to recognize the thousands of negative thoughts run through our minds. A better way is to be aware of your emotions.

If you feel an emotion that just doesn't feel good, it's an indicator that you are thinking negative thoughts. When you notice you are feeling anything other than good, instead counter it by choosing a new thought that makes you feel better emotionally. It is a deceptively simple and "common-sense" approach to life, but very few people actually recognize the perfect beauty of this approach to life. You'll know you're on the right track when you feel good most of the time.

> "When you jettison all money fears, you instantaneously become magnetic to money. I now believe your bank balance reflects the ratio of fears vs. confidence you have about money."
> – Dan Kennedy

This quote really speaks to financial wealth, which is not the same as prosperity, but I included it here because I do think it's an important quote and an important point. Since many people do equate financial success with prosperity, it is important to recognize all of the psychological factors that limit us from fully realizing our true income potential. Any feelings of fear, whether they are centered around money or something else, are barriers to realizing abundance and prosperity.

As Kennedy says, when you jettison fears (on any subject) you become magnetic, and begin to attract into your life everything that you have wanted. This is another way to describe the Law of Attraction. So it is important to be clear with ourselves about what we are fearful about, and work to move through the fears.

> "The human race has had long experience and a fine tradition in surviving adversity. But we now face a task for which we have little experience, the task of surviving prosperity."
> – Alan Gregg

As a nation, the United States has experienced tremendous prosperity since World War II, but ironically, as a whole, people are less satisfied, less in tune with themselves and each other, and are feeling less prosperous. National financial prosperity has only seemed to inflame the desire for more financial prosperity. But people in general do not recognize themselves as being prosperous because a sense of financial prosperity is all relative.

If we continually compare ourselves to someone with more financial wealth, we will always sense a lack. Recognize your incredible standard of living. Take time to stop and smell the roses. Appreciate your freedom, and the loved ones in your life. Prosperity abounds the moment you lift your gaze and shift your intention to feeling blessed by everything that is already in your life.

"Divine Love always has, and always will meet, every human need."
– Mary Baker Eddy

In this quote, Mary Baker Eddy (the first and only female founder of a worldwide religion – Christian Science) affirms that the intelligence that formed the universe made us in its image and likeness, and is an ever present source of help. This intelligence can be relied on to ensure our needs are met.

While having your basic needs being met is not the same as unbridled prosperity, if you don't have this fundamental trust in the benevolence of the universe, then you have no foundation on which to build greater abundance and prosperity. If you believe your creator, or the energy that is the source of the universe, can leave you "out there" on your own, without even your basic necessities being met, then how can you have any trust in ever achieving real or permanent prosperity?

> "Be thankful for what you have; you'll end up having more. If you concentrate on what you don't have, you will never, ever have enough."
> – Oprah Winfrey

Oprah, by anyone's measure, has a solid grasp on prosperity! Though she came from very humble beginnings and faced abuse and hardships as a child, she has always demonstrated gratitude for what she has, while striving for more.

She embodies both of the ideals of gratitude and prosperity, and therefore is one of the best living examples of someone who truly "gets it". Here she stresses the importance of gratitude and proper focus as prerequisites to greater prosperity.

> "If we really love ourselves, everything in our life works."
> – Louise L. Hay

This quote could be an entire book unto itself. Self-love is an absolutely critical ingredient to a rich life filled with the best of everything, and most importantly – peace of mind. You cannot have peace of mind, which could be considered to be a synonymous with prosperity, without healthy self-love. If you sense that you are lacking in this area, begin at once to focus on it. Louise Hay's books are an excellent place to begin.

> "No one lives long enough to learn everything they need to learn starting from scratch. To be successful, we absolutely, positively have to find people who have already paid the price to learn the things that we need to learn to achieve our goals."
> – Brian Tracy

If we want to accomplish much in life, and have great financial wealth, we must become highly educated in many areas, as well as become a person that is capable of handling the responsibility and power that comes with great wealth. Here Tracy points out that life is simply not long enough to learn it all on your own – you must study the books and lives of people whom you admire and trust.

Don't overlook the importance of continuous education, and modeling what has worked for others in our field or who have accomplished what we want to accomplish. The "life lessons" that took one person a lifetime to obtain can be read, understood (and hopefully integrated into your "life approach"), in just a few short hours.

No man ever achieved worthwhile success who did not, at one time or another, find himself with at least one foot hanging well over the brink of failure."
– Napoleon Hill

We have all faced failure, some greater than others, but no one is a stranger to failure. And the larger, more audacious the risk that was taken, the greater is the chance for failure. But failure builds character, builds resolve, and therefore is one of the single most valuable teachers we will ever encounter. Instead of looking on failure as something to be avoided, realize that if you aren't failing with regularity, you probably are "playing it safe" in your life.

Take chances, dream big, put your neck on the line, and grow as a result. While unpleasant at times, failure has it's rightful place and value. As Napoleon Hill liked to say: "Every adversity, every failure, every heartache carries with it the seed of an equal or greater benefit."

"Learning is the beginning of wealth. Learning is the beginning of health. Learning is the beginning of spirituality. Searching and learning is where the miracle process all begins."
– Jim Rohn

Learning by its nature is asking for knowledge, for more. And nothing of value comes to us unless we ask, whether verbally or inwardly. Because the first act in the manifesting process is ASKING, an orientation toward continual learning is a prerequisite, and once engaged, it unleashes the forces that bring about our desires.

"As a well-spent day brings happy sleep, so a life well spent brings happy death."
– Leonardo DaVinci

No matter how prosperous or how shabby a life we lead, there comes the point where we all exit. And as the saying goes, you can't take it with you! While no-one "in body" can speak authoritatively on the final parting moment, certainly a well-lived life will leave a person free of major regrets.

No one should look back on their life with regret, because we all do the best that we can do, at that time. Making a conscious attempt to live life to its fullest is surely the best thing a person can do to ensure the moments leading up to the transition are moments of gratitude and peace of mind.

"Nine requisites for a contented life: Health enough to make work a pleasure. Wealth enough to support your needs. Strength enough to battle with difficulties and overcome them. Grace enough to confess your sins and forsake them. Patience enough to toil till some good is accomplished. Charity enough to see some good in your neighbor. Love enough to move you to be useful and helpful to others. Faith enough to make real the things of God. Hope enough to remove all anxious fears concerning the future."
– Johann Wolfgang von Goethe

These nine characters, sufficiently developed, are all any person needs to experience a contented life, one full of overflowing abundance. Meditating deeply on any of these nine characteristics, and how well you reflect them, will put you on the path to prosperity.

A good practice is to consider each of these characteristics for one week. Do not belittle yourself if you feel that you fall short in some of these areas (because we all do), but instead consider how well you already live each one. Imagine how great you'll feel about your personality after just a few months of working to manifest these traits in your day to day behavior.

> "Small opportunities are often the beginning of great enterprises."
> – Demosthenes

Many people let seemingly lesser opportunities pass them by because they are looking to become the next Bill Gates. But nearly every large enterprise that creates wealth for thousands of people begins as a small idea. Never underestimate the power of a small idea, coupled with an intense desire. No good idea, no matter how small, is "beneath you".

Better to move forward with a small idea than to sit by idly waiting for a momentous breakthrough. An opportunity is an opportunity, and you can always choose to change course later of to choose a new path altogether.

> "All achievements, all earned riches, have their beginning in an idea."
> – Napoleon Hill

Everything that we see around us once began as an idea in mind or Mind. Ideas are the starting point of everything. Don't overlook the utterly simple yet glorious nature of an inspired idea.

When we feel inspired by an idea, we are in alignment with prosperity. The more you can stay with the feeling of inspiration, you are changing your predominant vibration to one of prosperity. The process is not difficult, and it should feel lighthearted in its own time.

Most people treat the present moment as if it were an obstacle that they need to overcome. Since the present moment is Life itself, it is an insane way to live."
– Eckhart Tolle

In the last two decades, there has been a renewed emphasis on the idea of attempting to focus exclusively in the present moment as a powerful spiritual practice. We may think back to the past, or project into the future, but the moments that make up our life are always happening "right here and right now". Focusing on being present in the moment brings richness to life which previously had gone without noticed.

The primary message of this book is that Prosperity can be felt and appreciated NOW, in under 30 seconds, by merely shifting your thinking and aligning your energy with that of what you want. Coming into alignment with what you want is a moment by moment process, always happening in THE NOW.

Feel your feelings now. Improve your feeling now. Enjoy things now. Appreciate all that you have right now. If you can't bring yourself to come face to face with right now, and appreciate it, prosperity will likely always elude you.

> "I try to learn from the past, but I plan for the future by focusing exclusively on the present. That's where the fun is."
> – Donald Trump

While "The Donald" is not usually considered a paragon of spiritual wisdom, the man does know a few things about how to live large, and have some fun - two major facets of abundance and prosperity. To most Americans in fact, he is the living definition of prosperity. He focuses intently on the present. And he practiced that before he made his first billion dollars.

While not born into poverty, and given some advantages in life, The Donald has mastered the concept of prosperity, and his life has been a testament to it ever since. Take his advice, focus on making the present as rich as possible in every way, and you will be rich in every way.

> "People often say that motivation doesn't last. Well, neither does bathing - that's why we recommend it daily."
> – Zig Ziglar

Zig Ziglar has led a long and very rich life, and has been a motivating force to tens of millions of people worldwide through very practical and "down-to-earth" motivational books and speeches. Zig's a funny guy, and here he brings it out by pointing out that motivation is not a "one time deal". Motivation is energy, and that energy must be cultivated, recharged, and recreated as needed to keep us moving forward.

Remember that action taken in a spirit of negativity produces little results. But action taken with joyous expectation multiplies a hundred-fold, and produces incredible results. When you motivation starts to wane, then pause and take note of your previous accomplishments and progress. Then refocus on your blessings, your goals, and recommit to having fun along the way. In this way motivation will be renewed.

How often to renew your motivation? Zig recommends renewing it about as often as you bathe.

> "All successful people are big dreamers. They imagine what their future could be, ideal in every respect, and then they work every day toward their distant vision, that goal or purpose."
> – Brian Tracy

Dreaming big is wonderful, but if you truly want to see all of your desires manifest in reality, you need to have a sense of vision. People who are good at envisioning their goals and the future they intend for themselves are 99% at their destination before they ever get started implementing their plan.

When you envision with strong positive emotion, the Universe, through the Law of attraction, will work with you to bring your vision to reality. It will require action on your part, but it will feel like floating downstream towards the goal, as opposed to swimming upstream against a strong current.

> "A positive mental attitude and definiteness of purpose is the starting point toward all worthwhile achievement"
> – Napoleon Hill

A positive mental attitude isn't a cure-all, but it is a prerequisite for any real forward progress, both in material terms and spiritual terms. When you have a vision, and idea, a goal, and a plan to get there, you have definiteness of purpose.

Combine the positive mental attitude with that definite purpose and you have a powerful combination that is sure to bear fruit. Your great attitude will keep you moving forward over the obstacles when they arise, and ensure you have the needed energy for the long haul.

"When you discover your mission, you will feel its demand. It will fill you with enthusiasm and a burning desire to get to work on it."
– W. Clement Stone

What is your mission? If you aren't sure, that is okay, but you should strive to discover it. Your mission is not written on a clay tablet somewhere, it is not predestined, and your mission is not to discover it. Just pick something that really excites you and go with it!

Your mission is whatever you decide it is, no matter what someone else tells you. You can always change your mind later. But it's important to decide and move forward on your mission, because the energy that you will feel once you discover it will propel you further and faster than anything else. Remember, it's hard to say no to someone on a mission!

"How can you become more prosperous?? INTEND IT!"
– from the movie *The Secret*

First and foremost, one must have the clear and strong intention to experience and enjoy true prosperity. This cannot be a passing wish or an idle daydream, but instead must be a persistent desire that is deeply rooted in your being. Once this is in place, experiencing prosperity is no longer a matter of *if*, it's a matter of *when*.

> "There is a cooperative Universe at your fingertips, ready and able to help you in more ways than you can begin to imagine..."
> – Abraham

It does not matter whether you use the term "Universe", "God", "Jesus", or "Source Energy", the principle is the same. Most people do not consider the Universe to be their divine benefactor, but it is. The Law of Attraction dutifully brings you whatever you desire, but what you truly desire is whatever you give your attention to, not what you merely say that you want.

Giving your attention to any object or situation it is proof that you are a match to it on the most basic level of simple vibration and energy. If you really want something different than what you have now, then prove it - by focusing on it exclusively, and see what your results are.

> "What I know is, is that if you do work that you love, and the work fulfills you, the rest will come."
> – Oprah Winfrey

Oprah clearly loves her work, and we can't argue with the results she has achieved. Most of us spend such a large portion of our waking hours focused on our work, that if we do not love our work, it is truly a waste of time – time that will never be recaptured.

So we have two options, change our work to something we love and that fulfills us, or change our attitude and perspective so that we appreciate and enjoy the work that we do. One is not better than the other. What matters is the end result, being happy and fulfilled by our work, and that energy will spill over into the rest of our day, and the rest of our lives.

"Any person who contributes to prosperity must prosper in turn." – Earl Nightingale

It is Universal Law. Contribute to prosperity of others, of society, and add value wherever you can, and you will in turn prosper spiritually and in all other aspects of life. But focus on the adding value part, and don't worry about the rewards aspect very much. Otherwise your contribution is tainted with a selfish energy, an energy of "need" that limits the natural benefits that you would have naturally accrued.

> "Somehow I can't believe that there are any heights that can't be scaled by a man who knows the secrets of making dreams come true. This special secret, it seems to me, can be summarized in four "Cs". They are curiosity, confidence, courage, and constancy."
> – Walt Disney

These four "Cs" apply to all of the aspects of prosperity. But you can begin to improve in all four of these qualities almost instantly. Reading these quotes whenever you feel doubtful or discouraged will get you in alignment with these qualities. And the moment you feel better about yourself, your abilities, and these four "C's", you will begin to attract more prosperity.

> "A man of character finds a special attractiveness in difficulty, since it is only by coming to grips with difficulty that he can realize his potentialities."
> – Charles de Gaulle

This sums up the idea of having an appreciation for contrast. I don't think anyone relishes the idea of dealing with circumstances that feel like the opposite of prosperity, but most of the difficulty is in our feelings, the resistance we put up to what is.

An awareness of how much we worry about, or attempt to avoid difficulty, is something we should strive to develop. If we drop the resistance, most of the difficulty goes away. But some circumstances, in the moment, are truly difficult for nearly everyone, and there are few people who can appreciate that "special attractiveness" presented by difficulties.

"It is literally true that you can succeed best and quickest by helping others to succeed."
– Napoleon Hill

Helping others may not appear to be the fast path to financial prosperity, but keep in mind that a) financial success is only one aspect of true prosperity, and b) there is no better, faster way to feel good about yourself than to render help or aid to someone who really needs it.

Someone who is dedicated to helping others succeed will themselves succeed for numerous reasons. The first is that in helping others, you will be in alignment with the idea of success and progress. Your own uplifted attitude will help them and help you, by keeping you secure in a spirit of generosity and prosperity.

Feeling gratitude and appreciation will be the natural result of helping others, and these will lead you toward your own success. And your generosity will be rewarded by those whom you have helped, and by that mysterious force best described as "you reap what you sow".

"If you want to change who you are, begin by changing the size of your dream. Even if you are broke, it does not cost you anything to dream of being rich. Many poor people are poor because they have given up on dreaming."
– "Rich Dad" from Robert Kiyosaki's Rich Dad, Poor Dad

Poor can be defined as a lack of wealth, and it can be defined as a broken spirit. Either way, it doesn't feel good. Dreaming big dreams, whether they ever come true or not, is a bold statement to the universe that you appreciate life, growth, and desire to expand. So dream big!

There is nothing wrong with wanting MORE. It is our fear that our more will be denied or withheld, that keeps us from dreaming big in the first place. In an ironic twist, those that seek to avoid the denial of more ensure their denial of it. Don't worry, it won't be denied you.

> "Appreciation is the absence of everything that feels bad and the presence of everything that feels good. When you focus upon what you want - when you tell the story of how you want your life to be - you will come closer and closer to the vicinity of appreciation, and when you reach it, it will pull you toward all things that you consider to be good in a very powerful way."
> – Abraham
> (from *Money, and the Law of Attraction*)

Appreciation is hard to feel when your life situation isn't optimal. But feeling "deep and abiding" appreciation is what is called for to see significant changes towards the manifestations that we usually associate with prosperity and abundance.

You can have feelings of prosperity and abundance the instant you choose to feel appreciation. When you've made that choice, your energy will shift. If you stay long enough with the feeling of appreciation, then your conditions and circumstances will start to change to bring you the physical equivalent of what you are feeling appreciation for.

Concluding Thoughts

Prosperity is a simple process and a continual state of being, and it all starts with feeling good. I hope these quotes have helped you invoke a sense of hope, general well-being, abundance, gratitude, expectation, and joy. If so, then in this moment, you are feeling what it feels like to be prosperous. Keep it going!

Do not underestimate the importance of feeling good, joyful, and feeling appreciation. It has more power than most of us realize. Return to these quotes as necessary to keep the flame of prosperity alive in you. Stay on the path!

Remember that feeling great in the moment does not mean you have agreed to stay at your current level. It doesn't mean that you have "settled" for less than what you know you are capable of achieving. But it does mean that you have chosen to be at peace with your present circumstances, even if you are experiencing challenging times.

It is the creative "act" of relaxing with the present circumstances, re-centering yourself based on your current desires, and then moving forward with

hope and positive expectation, which creates the energy flow that will propel you forward out of the present circumstances. Follow this process and soon you have more physical evidence of prosperity and abundance to match the inner sense of it that you've been cultivating by reading these quotes.

Take action only when you are feeling the spirit of prosperity. To take action at any other time is of little use. A combination of wanting more, expecting more, and joyously carrying out your duties, tasks, and plans, is what prosperity is, and feeling it *now* ensure feeling much more of it in the future.

Don't be afraid to want, and don't judge what you want. Wanting more is a wonderful thing, and because we are all growing, expanding, and adding to "all that is", getting and experiencing more is guaranteed. So relax, figure out what you want, allow the pleasant, relaxed, patient anticipation to settle over you. Revel in it, and enjoy the moment. String together enough of these types of moments and you will have created an incredible life for yourself!

Recommended Resources

For free weekly podcasts and online interviews with prosperity experts that will get you motivated, energized, and feeling prosperous, visit: **www.ProsperityRadio.com**

To learn more about working with a personal prosperity coach to experience abundance, health, wealth, peace of mind, and achieve your goals, visit: **www.ProsperityRadio.com/Coaching**

Learn the secret behind *The Secret,* and the true meaning of the Law of Attraction and the Art of Allowing, visit: **www.Abraham-Hicks.com**

Breathe! What would happen if one million people breathed synchronously? An excellent website to help you get centered and focused, visit: **www.DoAsOne.com**

To find a group of like-minded people in your area to exchange ideas in any subject or interest and expand your social comfort zone, visit: **www.Meetup.com**

Book layout and cover design by Sabrina Harris. You can contact her at **sabrina.harris@gmail.com**

ABOUT RYAN A. HARRIS

Ryan A. Harris is a professional speaker, author, and prosperity coach. In addition, he is a marketing consultant and copywriter to the information technology, real estate, professional development, medical spa, and anti-aging industries.

Through his marking consulting and copywriting services, teaches how to profitably get new customers, get existing customers to spend more money, and how to maximize revenue by streamlining internal business processes.

Ryan has co-authored two books on marketing for the medical spa industry, is the co-founder of the Medspa Marketing Institute, and is the host of Prosperity Radio.

He is also the author of the forthcoming book "Conquering a Financial Crisis" and he lives in beautiful San Diego, California, and enjoys learning from his 4 year old son, Ryder.

www.ingramcontent.com/pod-product-compliance
Lightning Source LLC
Chambersburg PA
CBHW071755040426
42446CB00012B/2574